To LaWana,

Thank you for sharing my story with your tea[...]

Hugs,

Debra Searle

The Journey

HOW TO ACHIEVE AGAINST THE ODDS

Shoal
Projects Ltd

DEBRA SEARLE

Published by Shoal Projects Ltd.
ISBN: 978-0-9556186-0-4

Design and page layout by Owen Jones
www.artboyart.com

Credits

Pictures: grateful acknowledgement is made to Express Newspapers, Chris Brandis, Tim Searle, Mark Pepper/ Marinepics.com, Sian MacFadyen, Carlisle Group and John Farnell.

For their kind permission to reproduce the New Radicals' lyrics, grateful acknowledgement is given to EMI Music Publishing Ltd, London WC2H 0QY.
'You Get What You Give' Words and Music by Gregg Alexander and Richard W Nowels Jr © 1998, Grosse Point Harlem Publishing/ EMI Blackwood Music Inc/ Future Furniture Music/ EMI April Music Inc, USA.

Grateful acknowledgement is made to The Times for their kind permission to reproduce the leading article from 28/01/2002. © The Times, NI Syndication Ltd, 28/01/2002.

Grateful acknowledgement is made to Ursula K. Le Guin for her kind permission to reproduce the 'Journey' quote on page 101.

Inside

Setting the Scene

On a warm June afternoon in 1966, a young Scotsman stood on the beach of a little finishing port near Cape Cod, Massachusetts. In the foreground was a small wooden rowing boat. Beyond stretched the vastness of the North Atlantic Ocean.

Ninety-two days later, Chay Blyth and John Ridgeway rowed the English Rose III towards the rugged coastline of Ireland after an epic adventure into the unknown. At 26 years of age Chay Blyth had successfully rowed the Atlantic, and this is where my story begins.

Three decades later, in celebration of his amazing Atlantic crossing, Chay Blyth had a madcap idea — to organise a rowing race across an ocean! At the time, more people had been to the moon than had rowed the Atlantic, but undeterred Chay gave life to the 1997 Atlantic Rowing Race. It was the first ever rowing race across an ocean. Double-handed teams set out from Tenerife in identical 24ft marine plywood rowing boats, to compete on equal terms over a 3,000 nm voyage, across the Atlantic Ocean to Barbados. Each team had to carry everything they needed to survive including a water maker, freeze-dried food, medical kit, solar panels and boat spares. Outside assistance would result in immediate disqualification.

The 1997 Atlantic Rowing Race had been intended as a one-off but after its success Chay Blyth saw no reason to end the story there. An east to west race across the Atlantic was planned for every four years and we were determined to be on that start line in 2001. So were a further thirty-five teams of competitors drawn from thirteen countries making it a truly international race.

Andrew and I were the only married team in the Atlantic Rowing Race, and the only mixed sex team in the event. We lined up against thirty-four double-handed mens teams and just one all female team off Playa San Juan Harbour, Tenerife on 7th October 2001.

An epic adventure of vast proportions unfolded over the subsequent four months — perhaps not as we had planned but an epic adventure - for both of us - none the less.

The journey held excitement, disappointment, disqualification, determination, exhilaration, peace, danger, loneliness and many hard, hard lessons. But somewhere along the journey something powerful happened — a personal realisation that I was capable of more. More hardship. More challenges. More joy. More determination. More attitude. More adaptability. More attainment.

My hope is that through the parables told within this small book you too will seek 'more'. And that you too might discover that the journey is as fulfilling as the journey's end.

DEBRA SEARLE
AUTHOR

The Journey Begins

Latitude 28° 06´ Longitude 16° 52´   ~   Distance to Barbados: 3375 nautical miles

the journey
BEGINS

Mother Nature delivered another blow, her briny waves slapping me across the face.

I spat out the salty water and shook my head, trying to remove the stinging salt from my eyes. She had been a graceful companion as we'd rowed away from Tenerife a few hours earlier, giving us an awe-inspiring start to our race across the Atlantic ocean to Barbados. But now her anger, in the watery form of the Atlantic, was roused.

As the winds picked up and the waves became ferocious I began to see a nervousness in Andrew that I had not witnessed before. The waves were breaking over the boat and although adrenaline prevented us from feeling tired, we felt helpless. We were both being violently sea sick. It was almost dark; we had lost control of the boat and didn't know what to do to regain it. Andrew looked lost.

We were entering the acceleration zone, where all the winds that have funnelled around the Canary Islands reunite, and were having our first taste of what life on the ocean in a small wooden rowing boat was really going to be like. We struggled on through the night, as the stormy conditions enveloped us, refusing to acknowledge that our attempts were futile against such power. Without moonlight it was impossible to see and respond to the waves. They were intermittently twice the height of the boat, hitting us from all angles and threatening to capsize us. It was our first experience of such conditions. We had little knowledge of, or confidence in, the boat's reactions. Training off the coast of England and Wales had ill-prepared us for what the Atlantic was now, literally, throwing at us. We were left with no choice but to abandon the rowing and take shelter in the tiny cabin, hoping that our deployed drogue would hold us stationary.

On the morning of day two, as light crept onto the horizon, we were able to survey the scene. It was apparent that conditions had not improved.

Andrew woke frustrated that we were still side on to the waves and was convinced that we were doing something wrong. He had found the first night horrendous, imagining that each slapping wave against the side of the cabin was the cracking noise of Troika Transatlantic breaking up.

Andrew was becoming paranoid, thinking we were the only crew caught in the rough conditions and that the other 35 teams must have gained hundreds of miles on us. We began to discuss the options, but not having any answers only increased Andrew's feelings of being out of control. I was optimistic and full of suggestions, but each one was greeted with an uncharacteristically negative response.

"I feel completely out of my depth." Andrew commented unhappily. "I didn't come out here to be thrown in all directions by the waves. I came out here to row and we aren't even able to do that in these conditions."
"The guys from the '97 race told us that the first five days are the hardest" I reminded him.
"I thought they said that getting to the start line was the hardest part!" Andrew snapped. "Now it's the first five days as well?"
"It will get better," I said. "After five days the sea sickness will have passed, we'll have found our sea legs and we'll be out of the acceleration zone."

I really hoped this was true, particularly the bit about the sea legs. At six foot five inches Andrew was far too big for the boat and was constantly colliding with everything. He was either going to break himself or the boat!

Andrew was quiet for the next few hours, obviously thinking everything through. When he finally responded he said, "Okay, let's give it a go for a few more days then we'll see how we feel".

The seasickness did not return after that first night, but Andrew still found he couldn't eat. On day three after another sleepless night I became increasingly concerned about lack of food and sleep and the effect that this was having on Andrew's ability to think straight. My emotions were in complete turmoil. I was desperately worried about Andrew. But the sun shone, I was surfing down waves and absolutely loving every minute of life at sea. It was hard to believe we could feel so differently about the same experience.

The Journey Begins

Latitude 28° 06′ Longitude 16° 52′　~　Distance to Barbados: 3375 nautical miles

But day eight was the big turning point from which there would be no way back.

Andrew spent the day trying to mend a leaky pump attached to the water maker. He grew more despondent as the hours passed, convinced that he was making the leak worse. He had lost confidence in his abilities and was increasingly self-deprecating. I had never seen this side of his generally stoical and optimistic character before. Perhaps he hadn't either. He had hardly eaten for a week and the weight loss had been dramatic. Panic attacks had prevented him from sleeping and the symptoms of malnutrition and sleep deprivation accelerated his paranoid state.

By the end of that evening heavy rain had begun to fall and the first signs of a storm were evident. I pulled on my Musto waterproofs and crawled through the hatch for my evening shift while Andrew rested in the cabin. I was uncomfortable with the thunder and lightning, but was determined to make the most of the fact that the heavy rain appeared to have flattened the surface of the water. The sheet lightning flashed out of the darkness, violently lighting up my watery 360-degree horizon and set my heart pounding. The low groan of distant thunder sounded like an animal in pain, putting me on edge in the tense moments before the inevitable crescendo.

When the lightning finally crashed it ricocheted across the surface of the water, vibrating in my lungs and left me cowering in the fleecy lining of my upturned collar.
At the end of my two-hour shift I crawled along the deck and sat outside the hatch. Not wanting to let the rain into the cabin I only opened it slightly.
I shouted over the sound of the rain, drumming on the roof of the cabin:
"Andrew, it's your turn."
Andrew didn't move. I wondered if maybe he hadn't heard me.
"Andrew." Still nothing. I tried some reassurance.
"It's not that bad out here if you put your Mustos on. It probably sounds worse than it is in the cabin with the rain drumming on the plywood."
He still didn't respond, but after the day he'd had, I figured that he probably needed a bit more encouragement.
"Why don't you put the head phones on under your hood and listen to some music while you row?" Nothing.
"Andrew?"
Still only slightly concerned, I stuck my head in further, and was shocked by what I saw. Andrew had curled his massive frame into the foetal position. He was groaning as if in pain and shaking violently from head to toe. He was obviously terrified.

I had tried encouraging, supporting and being there for him, but it just was not helping. I wondered if maybe I should try being firm.

"Andrew. I need your help," I pleaded – and then, with an irony I couldn't have appreciated, "I can't row this boat to Barbados on my own. We're a team. We have to work together." I watched him for a moment, his body still shaking, numb and unresponsive. I knew he wouldn't make it.

"Well if you aren't going to help, I guess I'll have to do it on my own." It was an unnecessary and low remark, made to force him into action. But it didn't. I returned to the oars for another two-hour shift, filled with frustration.

Why couldn't Andrew love it out here? I wanted to shout at him to snap out of it and pull himself together, even though deep down I knew he couldn't. I knew too, that fear can't simply be clicked on and off like a switch. I felt so terribly sad that he had struggled so far and that I was unable to make it better for him.

Two hours later nothing had changed, except that I was now exhausted. I stripped my sopping clothes into a bin liner and crawled into the cabin next to Andrew. There was no point trying to talk. He had not responded for hours. I realised it would be better to wait until we had both rested.

I woke at five-thirty and found Andrew lying on his back, staring at the ceiling of the cabin with wide eyes. It was hard to believe that I was looking at the same person that I had witnessed curled in a ball just a few hours before. There was a serenity about him, almost a peacefulness. Something had changed.

"I can't go on." His voice was calm and controlled. I realised in that moment that he had stopped fighting the fear and had finally given in. That was the source of his peacefulness.

He sounded as if he had been considering his decision all night, but as he said the words I watched a tear roll down the side of his face.

"It's okay." I said softly. "I know." I had known from the minute I had stuck my head through the hatch the previous night and had seen Andrew in a place where he should never have been — way out beyond his fear threshold. It was the right decision — the only decision.

I understood his tears of frustration. We had spent years planning our race entry, raising the funds, building the boat and getting ourselves prepared for the challenge. He had accepted that he had to give up on our dream and it was devastating for him. I longed to take away his pain. Such a big decision wasn't going to be an easy one to live with.

THE JOURNEY
[HOW TO ACHIEVE AGAINST THE ODDS]
Run the Movie
Latitude 24° 25′ Longitude 21° 01′ ~ Distance to Barbados: 2467 nautical miles

run THE movie

I suppose the decision to carry on alone should have been a difficult one for me . . . but it wasn't.

I was loving life at sea and that was obvious to both of us. Andrew had never seen me looking so positive and in control. My enthusiasm was shatterproof. No matter how bad it got I seemed to thrive. Despite Andrew's concern for my safety he didn't want to stop me from fulfilling my dream, so he encouraged me wholeheartedly to row on alone.

My head and my heart told me I had to give it a go.

For as long as I can remember I have always wanted to be a professional adventurer. After completing a five day expedition as part of my Gold Duke of Edinburgh's Award at school I began to read books by explorers such as Ranulph Fiennes and other brave men who had tackled Everest or canoed the mighty rivers of the world. My school careers advisor didn't think it was the best idea she had ever heard but I had become passionate about all things adventurous and set my heart on becoming a 'female Ranulph Fiennes'! Life would have been a whole lot less dangerous and less stressful for my parents if I had grown up with a passion for accounting or beauty therapy but I didn't.

This was what I loved doing more than anything else and, delightfully, I discovered that I had quite a gift for living in very uncomfortable conditions and for putting my mind and body through tough times.

But the decision to carry on alone, armed with the knowledge that it may take the support yacht up to two weeks to get to me if I injured myself or capsized the boat, put this adventure on a whole different level to any I had tackled previously. I had never even spent one day alone in my entire life, let alone tackled a solo expedition, so I knew I had to face up to some big questions about whether my heart would still be in it if there was no one else around to watch my back and help me through the hard times.

Thinking back to something Sir Chay Blyth said at our pre-race briefing helped seal the decision to carry on alone. Chay (who rowed the Atlantic with John Ridgway in 1966 and was the Race Organiser) had said to us all.

"As you are rowing across the Atlantic looking down at your little brown toes, ask yourself, 'Am I the happiest I could possibly be?'" CHAY BLYTH

After Andrew and I made the decision for him to be rescued I asked myself Chay's question: "am I the happiest I could possibly be?". I pulled on the oars and drove back with my legs, taking a good look down at my exceptionally brown toes out in front of me on the foot place and I was thrilled that my answer was a resounding 'yes!'. That my heart was still most definitely in it was all the confirmation I was looking for.

As for the head bit, well that had been engrained with a vision of life alone at sea some four years earlier when I read of an amazing solo rower called John Searson. John had rowed the Atlantic single-handed after his rowing partner was forced to retire with a back injury. Not only was I inspired by his phenomenal solo voyage but it impressed on me the need to be prepared for any eventuality — even the possibility of Andrew having to be rescued, leaving me with the decision to carry on alone or quit.

After reading an account of John's journey I decided that if Andrew was forced to retire from the race through injury then I would at least give it a go on my own, as John had. That promise to myself had remained buried in the back of my head throughout the years as we prepared for the race. Being mentally prepared for the possibility that one of us may get injured made the decision to carry on alone so much easier. In fact, to keep that promise to myself, there really was no decision to be made. I only gave myself one option — to go on alone and finish it for both of us.

However, what we hadn't realised when we made the call for the rescue at the end of the first week was that it was going to be another full week before the safety yacht would get to us. By day 13 I had secured, fixed and rearranged everything that would make life safer and easier for me as I continued solo. Little rowing had been achieved. The waiting game continued.

From the dawn of day 14 we were on the lookout for the distinctive pale yellow sails of the safety yacht on the horizon. The mood was a mixture of sadness and excitement for both of us. Andrew was excited to be getting off Troika Transatlantic and I was excited about my new solo adventure — but we hated the thought of being apart. At times Andrew seemed distant. The emotional battle must have been tough for him to deal with. I couldn't decide which of my emotions was dominating: the excitement of embarking on my new solo adventure, the sadness of being separated from Andrew or the relief of knowing he was finally going to be safe and well.

We first spotted the yacht at 1pm.

Trying to find a rowing boat in the Atlantic is like spotting the proverbial needle in a haystack. Even when a yacht is only half a mile away, a rowing boat can be almost impossible to find, as it is constantly lost amongst the waves. It took the yacht crew a further two hours until 3pm to locate us. We finally made radio contact on the VHF and were left with 20 minutes alone before they would draw alongside. It was time to say our goodbyes.

Andrew sat outside the cabin, with his little bag packed, all ready to go: "Just remember, if it doesn't work out, or if anything happens, we'll be right back to get you".

"I know. I'll probably hate being on my own but I've got to try. I'll always wonder 'what if' if I don't give it a go."

"You will stay clipped in, won't you?"

"Yep."

Andrew gave me a big hug, "I'm going to miss you," he muffled, his face buried into my hair.

"I'll miss you too."

We held each other and cried.

Andrew's anguish was obvious: "I don't want to leave you now."

"I don't want you to either."

There was something rather ominous about watching the safety yacht gliding slowly through the water towards us, its yellow sail apparently growing larger. It looked like the fin of a giant shark. This, I mused, was the thing that was going to be responsible for taking my husband away from me.

Mentally I knew I was ready. I had spent the week doing visualisation exercises to prepare myself. They are the one thing I can rely on to help me feel more in control during life's more intense moments. I have found that in any intense situation, be it at home, at work or during an expedition, the most effective visualisation exercise for me is a technique I call 'Run the Movie', where I run a movie in my head of the impending moment. I see the scene unfolding and imagine experiencing it through every sense in my body — smells, sounds, colours, the things someone might say or do and how I will respond, along with how I am going to feel. Every second unfolds in minute detail. I sometimes play the same movie over and over again, viewing different versions of conversations or events and every time my performance is an Oscar winning performance! In the movie I have all the right answers and handle the situation in the scene in just the right way.

I'm not a great fan of horror movies but the few times I have watched them I have noticed that my 'run the movie' technique has exactly the same effect as watching a horror movie for a second time. The first time you put the DVD in the machine and press play you find yourself jumping at the scary bits because you don't quite know what is going to happen or when. But when you put the DVD in for a second viewing and press play you don't jump when you get to the scary bits because you know when they are coming and are prepared for them.

By running movies in my head I am effectively preparing myself for the scary scenes in life so that when the impending moment arrives I don't jump. I've seen it before in my head and am prepared for any eventuality. From time to time I think we all feel fear because we don't know what is going to happen next or how we are going to cope in a given situation but I have found that if I can visualise some of the possibilities then I can limit or even eliminate the fear. This, in turn, makes me feel more in control and has the knock on effect of helping me to perform better.

So that is all I did when Andrew left the rowing boat. I just pressed play and the movie started to run.

Burn It As Fuel

Latitude 24° 33′ Longitude 20° 54′ ~ Distance to Barbados: 2301 nautical miles

burn IT AS fuel

We would never have predicted the way things turned out.

Neither would our friends and acquaintances who all knew of Andrew's pedigree as a successful oarsman. They believed it was me who would struggle at sea, and often made comments to Andrew, suggesting that if he was really serious about winning the race he should go with another man. It never helped my cause when they discovered that I had not rowed prior to entering the Atlantic Rowing Race! We were both amazed by the responses we received when we told people we were entering the Race together. The passing comments and stunned looks we received said it all, especially when we talked to other rowers.

A conversation we had at Henley Royal Regatta was a prime illustration of this pervading attitude. Andrew introduced me to an old rowing acquaintance of his in the Fawley Bar. My friend Joanna King was also with us, and the conversation turned to the Atlantic Rowing Race.

"Who are you rowing with?" asked the six-foot-five-inches (1.95m) tall acquaintance - himself a rower.

"My wife." Replied Andrew, looking Mr Six-foot-five straight in the eyes at matching height.

Mr Six-foot-five immediately turned to Joanna, who is a 6ft lean 'rowing-goddess' of a woman, assumed she was Andrew's wife and started asking her about the race. I was ignored. Standing at five-foot-five (1.65m) the conversation was all taking place way above my head anyway, and I began to feel like a stupid little girl.

"Jo's not my wife" Andrew said, relieving an embarrassed Joanna. "This is my wife." He gestured proudly downwards to my less significant stature. The look on Mr Six-foot-five's face was a picture. It was a mixture of utter disbelief and brazen disgust. After what seemed like an eternity he finally gestured towards Joanna and said:

"Well, mate, if you're going to row the Atlantic with a woman you should at least go with one this size".

The disbelief in my ability continued right up to the point that Andrew sailed away on the safety yacht but the few weeks in Tenerife leading up to the start of the race were definitely the worst. They seem funny now but at the time some of the comments from the other teams were hard to swallow. For example, one young lady who was a family member of one of the other rowers asked me if I would be rowing or if I was going along to do the cooking and cleaning!

Although I laugh now, at the time I was getting pretty sick of it. Enduring endless looks and comments, all of which suggested that I was not big enough, strong enough or in any way skilled enough, began to play on my self-confidence.

I'm someone who used to find it very easy to waste time and emotional energy worrying about things I could not change but my time in Tenerife put a stop to that. It became apparent that I could not change what they thought of my participation in the race, or that I was the smallest competitor with the least rowing experience, so there was simply no point in wasting time and energy worry about it or letting it squash my confidence.

I decided it was time to be proactive rather than reactive so I took every negative comment and stored them all away in the back of my head.

I used to think 'when I get out there in those 30 foot waves I am going to think of you and what you just said to me and I'm going to burn it as fuel'.

Now I love looking back on this time in Tenerife as it is such a powerful reminded to me to focus on the things I can change rather than those things I can't.

When the safety yacht finally reached us they asked me to come on board the yacht briefly to sign a disclaimer. Andrew and I sat down with the skipper Jonathan in the galley and talked through the problems Andrew had been having.

Then we discussed how I would cope on my own.

Burn It As Fuel

Latitude 24° 33' Longitude 20° 54' ~ Distance to Barbados: 2301 nautical miles

HOOD C 24

Ward E

ROWING CHALLENGE

I couldn't be certain, but deep down I had this belief that I would be able to cope with the journey ahead, so I gave Jonathan an outline of the plans I had been visualising to ensure I would be safe.

"I'm going to make safety my number one priority, obviously." I explained. "I'll stay clipped into my harness if it's rough and always at night."

"We have that policy on the Challenge Yachts - it's a good one to stick to." said Jonathan. "You have to remember that if a wave washes you overboard, the wind would push the boat away faster than you could swim after it."

"I realise that. I've got a flare and the EPIRB (Emergency Position Indicating Radio Beacon) just inside the cabin hatch and we've moved the life raft to the foot well so that it's on deck and accessible."

Jonathan seemed reassured.

"It sounds like you've thought this through carefully and logically."

"We have." I nodded. "We feel certain we're doing what's best for both of us. I really want to give it a go."

Jonathan smiled, "I'm sure you'll do great Debs, but if you don't, just let Race HQ know and we'll be right back."

He grinned at an afterthought. "We've got a DVD player on board, hot showers, stereo, proper food and all the mod cons so we can look after you well if you do decide to give up."

I had no intention of giving up.

I don't think that the race organisers truly believed I could make it on my own so I was grateful to them for letting me try. They actually had good reason to believe that I would not be able to make the 3000 nautical mile journey solo, as two of the double-handed men's crews had already been reduced to one rower and had tried and failed in their solo bids. It was understandable to therefore conclude that I too would not be able to manage the solitude.

However what mattered was that I believed I could make it and I really did.

The sight of Andrew looking so relaxed on the safety yacht was a great relief. The shadow of fear in his eyes had already lifted and the muscles of his face, tightened by stress, had relaxed. Sian, the race nurse, was immediately on hand to help Andrew and that, too, was very comforting in our time of need. I looked forward to having the old Andrew back again. At times I had hardly recognised the man who had been onboard the rowing boat with me for 14 days.

Andrew had been too unwell to row for most of his time on Troika Transatlantic which resulted in us being the most easterly boat in the fleet. The safety yacht had the tall order of having to drop by all of the other rowing boats, firstly to check that they were alright but secondly to make sure that they weren't breaking any of the race rules. By coming to our assistance they were now quite some distance from the front-runners in the race and if they didn't sail after them straight away they wouldn't be able to catch up with the lead boats. Consequently the safety yacht was not able to take Andrew back to Tenerife.

In many ways I was pleased that the yacht had to push onwards as it meant Andrew would arrive in Barbados by sea after all. He would be with a professional crew, on a big, safe, comfortable yacht and with good medical support. It would be an achievement in its own right. Andrew was told that after a day resting he would be integrated into the crew watch rotation and become part of the race safety team. He looked forward to it.

I just didn't feel right on the yacht. Something about the way the tons of steel moved heavily through the water made me feel queasy. The motion just wasn't the same as the rowing boat. I had to get off before I was sick! I couldn't wait to get back on Troika and took that desire as confirmation that I had made the right decision.

Once the disclaimer was written and signed, I was eager to begin my new adventure. Up on deck, the atmosphere was light and happy, as I said my good byes to the crew. They teased Andrew that it was his turn to cook that night. He was in good hands and I felt certain that the banter on board would be a great thing to help Andrew through what had been an extremely heavy-hearted time.

I gave him a big hug and he whispered, "Good luck" in my ear. We had said everything we needed to say. It was time.

I climbed over the rail and lowered myself into the tender, while one of the crew steadied it, holding onto the side of the hull. We cast off and were on our way back towards my beautiful little Troika. I looked straight ahead. There was no turning back now.

My mind was made up.

shifting
COMFORT ZONES

As Andrew sailed away I didn't know what to do with myself . . .

. . .so I did what I always do and called my twin Hayley using the onboard satellite phone. Our conversation was typical of those we'd had throughout our childhood and teenage years, with Hayley, the (ten minutes) older and wiser one giving reassurance to her 'little' sister.

"Hayley, it's me."

"Hi Little One. Has the yacht reached you yet?"

"Yes – and it's left. I'm watching Andrew sailing away now."

"What are you doing talking to me? At least wait until you're really alone!"

"I didn't know what to do with myself."

"You feeling okay?"

"I'm fine. Actually I'm feeling really positive . . . excited."

"That's good. You'd better start rowing then."

"Okay."

"Call me later, after it is dark, if you get scared."

"Thanks Hayley–Bailey."

I took up the oars.

Those first few strokes on my own felt good. I kept looking over my shoulder at the yacht carrying Andrew away as it became an increasingly small sail in the distance. It seemed almost surreal. When it finally disappeared over the horizon I said to myself, "Well, here I am, on my own in a small rowing boat in the Atlantic".

I knew that the first day alone would be fine but was unsure how I would cope with the nights. I'm quite scared of the dark so I was expecting the first night to be a challenge, but there were considerably less heart palpitations than I had anticipated. I had a sense of invincibility that I hoped would last for all the nights to follow, a feeling largely developed after days of running the movies in my head. I had spent hours rehearsing positively that I would be strong and invincible on my own and that mental rehearsal was paying dividends.

In 1998 and 1999 I had represented Great Britain at the European and World Championships in Dragon Boat Racing. The skills I learnt with the GB squad proved to be very useful at sea. Our coach, Griff, had taught us how to take on a new persona to illicit a positive mental state. He would encourage us to take on pseudonyms like 'Fighting Tiger' to conjure up feelings of power and rid us of our weaker every-day labels. So, I was transformed from 'Debra the rower' into 'Debra - Warrior of the Waves'! Whenever I took on this pseudonym I always pictured a woman in the boat who looked more like the actress who plays 'Xena Warrior Princess' on the TV programme, rather than little wifey Debra who had never rowed before. Xena is an Amazonian looking woman in leather combat clothes with bulging muscles. I remember thinking that Griff was bonkers when he first suggested this and initially it did not help me much. It takes a bit of practice but it is amazing how you really can start to lock into the power within you by using this technique.

That evening I struggled to keep the boat straight in the waves. A wave caught Troika at an odd angle and tipped her up. I was thrown from my rowing seat against the safety wire and my neck took the bulk of the force against the taunt plastic covered metal line. I immediately developed a headache and had to crawl into the cabin to lie down.

I realised that if something serious had happened there would have been no one to help me. If I had been knocked unconscious the race HQ would not have known to send a safety yacht. But there was no point dwelling on the 'what ifs'. I understood the risks and simply had to keep running the movies to mentally rehearse for any eventuality. The safety yacht was still relatively close, but I knew there were times ahead when it wouldn't be. Mid-Atlantic it could take them up to two weeks to get to me. It was time to start fending for myself. I had never felt so in control of my own life.

Sadly that feeling did not last and by day two I was having to face up to my new life as a solo rower. There was just so much change to deal with. Not only was there the enormous change of losing Andrew and our team having halved but I also had to deal with taking on every role in the boat and change all of the two man systems so that just one person could manage them.

I couldn't even continue with our shift system of two hours on the oars, followed by two hours resting. Without Andrew to row for two hours while I was on a rest period I lost too many miles, so I changed to a two-hours-on, one-hour-off shift system leaving the boat to drift. But to try to get all of the jobs done in one hour, such as fixing the water maker, plotting my course on the chart, setting the GPS, cooking some food to eat and going to the toilet, it only left about 20 minutes to sleep in each one hour rest period. Consequently the change in our team caused a considerable amount of sleep deprivation, stress, apprehension and frustration at times, not to mention the doubling of my workload. The net result was finding myself outside of my comfort zone on a daily basis.

It is such a challenge to see the opportunities in changing situations, whether it's a change in our role at work or something in our home life, because change inevitably seems to put us outside of our comfort zone. The change in our team and consequently my life inside that boat put me so far over my pain and fear thresholds on many occasions and that was not a comfortable place to be. But there eventually came a turning point in the journey when I realised that the comfort zone seemed to be shifting to where I was. As I grappled with yet another big change onboard the boat I was often terrified or frustrated at the beginning but after I had done it a few times I got used to it and it became quite within the realms of my abilities. Initially it hadn't seemed like it would but I realised that if I stuck at it through the uncomfortable bit the comfort zone always shifted to where I was. Eventually that new role or task became the norm and then I could really start to excel, rather than just survive.

There is something very empowering about completing a new task, especially when the task seemed impossible beforehand. Initially I felt I had a limit to what I was able to achieve but I was wrong. The only limits to what we can do are the limits that we set for ourselves and I had been setting too many for too long. I grew so much by smashing those preconceived limits I had set for myself. It made me develop new skills in a super quick time — because I had to. With each success, in the way

I dealt with another big change, came a huge rush of confidence that I could harness to help me deal with the next big change and the next big challenge. I'm not saying it was easy because it was horrendous at times, but it gave me an openness to being outside of my comfort zone, and a determination to stick with it until the comfort zone shifted to where I was.

I didn't want the growing to stop when I got back from the Atlantic, so at work I started to force change to be able to create new opportunities to grow, both personally and corporately. It has allowed us to push the limits of what we thought we were able to achieve and resulted in new clients, in new industry sectors, along with roles and responsibilities that would otherwise have seemed way beyond our reach.

I am convinced that a positive attitude to change and an acceptance of that period of time outside of the comfort zone can be contagious in the work place. The more I am like this, the more it has rubbed off on those I work with. The reverse is also true. If you see new changes and challenges as a negative thing then so will everyone else around you. Okay, it might make things a little stressful for a while but the comfort zone always shifts — eventually.

Know Your Sharks!

Latitude 22° 58' Longitude 22° 42'   ~   Distance to Barbados: 2066 nautical miles

KNOW YOUR sharks!

Progress was painfully slow at this stage but I didn't mind.

Most days I was too busy revelling in the peace and tranquillity to worry about how slowly I was going, but the days when I rowed into a headwind were frustrating and physically draining. My hands and back always took the brunt of them. It wasn't blisters on my hands that were the problem, but stiffness.

Getting out of the cabin at 5.30am and taking those first few strokes into the headwinds was dark and miserable. Every muscle in my body would scream for mercy as I attempted to propel the boat into what felt like a brick wall. When I stopped for a rest, I would be blown back the single mile it had just taken me an hour to gain. It was hard not to get demoralised.

While having dinner one night I watched some rather large fish doing laps of the boat obviously enjoying swimming in the glow of my navigation light. At first, it was reassuring to have them there. I figured they would be unlikely to play around so casually if any sizeable 'Beasties from the Deep' were nearby. They stayed with me as I rowed into the night until a significant 'Beastie', maybe 6ft long, joined them.

I had previously been eagerly awaiting the return of the moon to lighten the darkness, but that night I wished it would go again. Moonlight reflects off the pale skin of the big 'Beasties' and makes them shimmer ominously under the surface of the water. When they swim fast they leave a trail of darting phosphorescence in their wake, like an underwater lightning bolt. It sparkles and twirls off their backs in bright yellows and greens.

Had the moon not been out I probably would not have noticed them. Ignorance can be bliss! As I watched each bolt of light hurtle towards the boat I hoped I was witnessing a dolphin rather than a shark, but my thinking was wishful.

My sole knowledge of sharks was based on what I had seen in the 'Jaws' movies as a youngster. I could not get the movie flashbacks of sharks gnawing through the side of boats out of my head. My apprehension was completely unnecessary and purely because I was armed with the wrong knowledge. As my journey progressed I learnt that sharks are graceful, intelligent creatures.

I have occasionally made the same mistake in meetings with sharks of the corporate variety. I ask myself "are you putting yourself in another shark situation here, Debra?", because that experience at sea taught me the necessity of investing time in researching the company, their competitors, their industry sector and, in particular, the senior directors or managers I am presenting to. Gaining that knowledge enables me to enter the meeting with a whole different level of confidence.

I've become an expert at hunting down in-depth information about people on Google! I'm always on the look out for that little gem — that name on the minutes of a local arts group or similar. I'm looking for that hint of a suggestion of what that person I am meeting with is most passionate about outside of their business life, so that I can somehow bring it into conversation and watch them open up.

Gaining the knowledge for me, as someone who finds selling or big meetings incredibly daunting, is a vital part of my preparation but I am always mindful of something I heard a preacher once say:

"Knowledge tells you that a tomato is a fruit but wisdom tells you not to put it in the fruit salad!"

During my rare moments of wisdom at sea I was able to reassure myself that sharks only attack if provoked, but this would lead me to a whole new line of concern over whether the splashing in and out of my oars could be provoking them. I began to lightly drop the blades into the water causing as little splash as possible – just in case.

Eventually I was so scared that I began having palpitations and scrambled for the cabin where I hid, petrified, until dawn. Stupid really. There was still only 6mm separating me from the Beasties in the water but because I could not see them I somehow felt calmer.

I knew I could not afford to miss so much of my night time rowing shifts hiding in the cabin so became transfixed on finding ways to cope with my fears and the never ending stream of dangers that I faced every day that threatened my confidence and reduced my productivity.

There were two sorts of dangers – the real dangers and the perceived dangers. The real ones were being run over by a ship while I was sleeping, hitting a half submerged container and ripping a hole in the bottom of the boat, being upturned by a whale or shark, being sunk in a storm . . . all those usual things one has to worry about on a daily basis! The perceived dangers were the same, except they weren't actually going to happen at that particular moment. I often imagined they were. In fact I convinced myself of them regularly but it was all in my imagination.

It may seem irrational but when you are alone in the dark, in a very small plywood boat, hundreds of miles from dry land, deprived of sleep and armed with the knowledge that it is going to take up to two weeks for help to get to you if you call for a rescue, it is hard to be rational about the dangers – whether they are real or not.

Issue by issue I broke down the problems and found a solution. For example, losing my nerve at night was often instigated by a sound. In the dark with minimal sight, other senses go into overdrive, particularly hearing. Every splashing wave raised my heart rate, but when I couldn't hear them the problem was eliminated.

So I started listening to loud music to help to block out the mysterious sounds of night. To stop myself searching for shapes in the waves, I would turn the music up and chant to myself "Look at the stars, look at the stars." If I saw an ominous shape in the water, I would throw my head back and look for a new constellation, while trying not to think about what might be swimming underneath the boat.

Even so, nothing could beat that moment when the light started to sneak on the horizon. As dawn approached it was hard not to feel reborn – as if the light of a new day was bringing with it a new vigour for life.

048   THE JOURNEY
       [HOW TO ACHIEVE AGAINST THE ODDS]
       Know Your Sharks!
       Latitude 22° 58' Longitude 22° 42'   ~   Distance to Barbados: 2066 nautical miles

I became increasingly reliant on music, and not just at night. Listening to it made each two-hour rowing shift enjoyable and helped it pass quickly. But it was more than that. It became a confidence booster and a way to regaining any lost motivation for the goal of crossing that big pond single-handed. There were about ten songs that had the ability to completely transform my mood. 'You Get What You Give' by New Radicals, particularly the line "don't give up", was the song I returned to time and time again. On listening to it I would feel my determination come creeping steadily back. It gave me a growing confidence that I was not going to be beaten by one bad day. It left me feeling empowered — like nothing was going to stand in my way.

Generally they were songs that linked to a happy memory or reminded me of the people I love — those special songs that we all have. I now have my special songs burnt onto a CD and as a playlist on my laptop and mp3 player. On the days when I hate my job and am being unnecessarily negative about everything I reach for that CD and, without fail, it lifts my mood and helps me to be the kind of person I would want to work with, rather than a grumpy old sod.

049

"But when the night is falling and you cannot find the light,
    when your dreams are dying – hold tight,
    you've got the music in you, don't let go, **DON'T GIVE UP**"

'You Get What You Give' by New Radicals

Choose Your Attitude

Latitude 21° 41´ Longitude 23˝ 23´   ~   Distance to Barbados: 1987 nautical miles

choose YOUR attitude

A few weeks after Andrew had been rescued I managed to accidentally row my way into the Cape Verde shipping lane.

Not only did I have head winds to deal with, I now had the added stress of dodging tankers and container ships. I was going back one nautical mile for every two forward. I couldn't help watching every nautical second that clocked on the GPS as I rowed sluggishly into the wind. Feeling like I had to really work for every inch of forward advancement, it was demoralising to then witness them slipping away as I drifted backwards when I stopped to rest. It was a frustrating game. The boat felt heavy in these conditions and caused much stiffness and aching the following day — but at least I was making some headway.

However, I was in to the swing of it and thoroughly happy. My contentment seemed to grow daily. Perhaps I had become too cocky because in an instant my world was turned on its head and all sentiments of calm left me. It left me breathless and wondering how everything could have gone wrong so quickly.

I had attempted to throw some of Andrew's powdered food over board as I didn't need it all and it weighed a vast amount. I needed to make the boat lighter to row. It was a blustery day and I wasn't thinking. If I had been, I would have realised that the powdered food would be dispersed everywhere by the wind. As I poured it over the side it blew up into my eyes, so I had to shut them tight. Once I could feel the container was empty I opened my eyes to see what resembled a scene from a winter wonderland. A film of white powder covered every surface, not only on the deck but in the cabin as the hatch was tied wide open.

It had coated my bed, clothes, pillow — everything. To make matters worse, the dried food did exactly what it is designed to do when mixed with water — it expanded rapidly! I wasn't too concerned about the deck. I could throw buckets of water over that and wash it out of the scuppers, but the inside upset me greatly. I tried pulling one of the foam pads that I slept on out of the cabin to brush off the powder but almost on command a wave splashed over the deck and hit the pad full on. Immediately the cushion started to sprout goo, like a bacteria growing rapidly out of control, doubling in size every second. I pushed the foam pad back inside, at first not noticing the water dripping off it onto the other pads. I felt like I couldn't win. Everything I did seemed to be making the situation worse. "Give me a break," I screamed at my sprouting bed.

I shut the hatch and turned my attention to getting the exterior sorted out first. As I struggled to clear up the deck, waves were landing on my head, soaking me to the skin. I had reached breaking point.

I looked up to take some deep breaths and count to ten to calm myself. I stopped at three, as my heart lurched. What I saw did nothing to induce calm. A huge container ship was bearing down on my position, its steel hull munching through the ocean between us.

The bow wave from the ship was being thrown 40 foot in the air, curling over in a mass of violently foaming white water. It was so close that there wasn't time for the captain to respond to a call on the VHF radio to make him aware of my existence.

In a moment of cutting fear I realised that even if the ship didn't hit me, the bow wave would tear the boat apart. Those on board the vast steel monster wouldn't hear the shattering of Troika's plywood hull over the thunderous noise of the engine, let alone my screams for help.

Surely this was it. Forget running the movie. I was going to die.

Seconds seemed like hours as the monster ploughed onward, slicing through the water. I stood motionless with fear, but as I looked closer at the bow wave, my distress began to ease. It might, it just might . . .

I realised with the beginnings of relief, that I could see the bow wave on the starboard side more than the port side wave. This meant that the ship was at an angle to Troika. Its course must have been a few degrees different to mine. A few life-saving-degrees. I realised it wasn't going to hit us. Troika could breathe easy. The ship would simply roar by, as if we were a speck in its eye.

I sat watching it pass, feeling mentally broken and alone. I felt helpless. Hopeless. The crew didn't even know I was there. I don't know how long I sat there without moving. Certainly long after the ship was out of sight.

My invincibility was gone.

I was overwhelmed in the aftermath of the terrifying emotions, and completely exhausted. I called my twin sister Hayley and told her that I was thinking about giving up and calling the safety yacht. I was crying so hard that I could hardly get the words out. I wanted to be home. I felt like I could not handle the pressure of fending for myself in such a vast ocean when there were dangers that were completely out of my control. Her reply was "Don't give up. You are capable of so much more mental and physical hardship than this". That one sentence was so powerful. I didn't know if I believed it at the time and frankly it was easy for her to say sat in her cosy office back in England. But the more I thought about it the more I realised she was right. I wasn't about to die, I wasn't in pain, I had food and I had water. She had given me hope.

After she had calmed me down she said,

"You know Debs, you've just got to choose your attitude."

We spoke at length about the truth that each one of us has the opportunity to choose the attitude we approach each new day with. An important part of my success was going to be connected to choosing a more positive attitude when faced with huge amounts of adversity.

I was going to be faced with many more life-threatening situations. More often than not I was going to have no control over the situation, as was the case with the ship. I could not change the situation but I could always change the way in which I was responding to it. You can always 'Choose Your Attitude'.

I fixed those three little words to the hatch in front of my rowing position so that I could focus on them throughout the day. At breakfast as I watched the sun rise, I would start by focusing on those three words: 'Choose Your Attitude'. It would have been so easy to sit at the oars being negative but it would have done me no good at all.

Choose Your Attitude has become more than just a motto to me — it is a way of life. I would make myself pick an attitude over breakfast every morning at sea but it had to be a positive one. Negative attitudes had been banned from onboard the rowing boat! I'd pick, say, 'optimism' as my attitude of the day then make myself list out loud all the things I could be optimistic about. I imagined seeing lots of great wildlife; achieving my best mileage to date; learning a few more Spanish verbs (I had 'Teach Yourself Spanish' CDs on board) or taking the time to be peaceful for a while.

By the end of breakfast I would feel pretty upbeat about what the day might bring, which in reality was crazy considering my circumstances. I was scared and could not sleep for more than 20 minutes at a time because I had to keep a look out for ships, super tankers and sharks that could end my life in an instant. I would row for days and make about 30 miles, then over one night I could be hit by a storm and lose it all and have to start again. Towards the end of my journey I had even run out of toilet paper and was using my sock! I was constantly on edge but refused to let myself dwell on how bad the situation was by making myself choose an appropriate attitude every morning, because that was the one thing I did have a choice about.

It helped me to have a trigger that reminded me to ask myself the question. It's so easy to forget to do it. I now have a new trigger as I don't have a hatch to look at. When I lock my car it goes 'beep, beep' and that is my trigger to ask myself the question . . . "come on Debra – which one is it going to be today?".

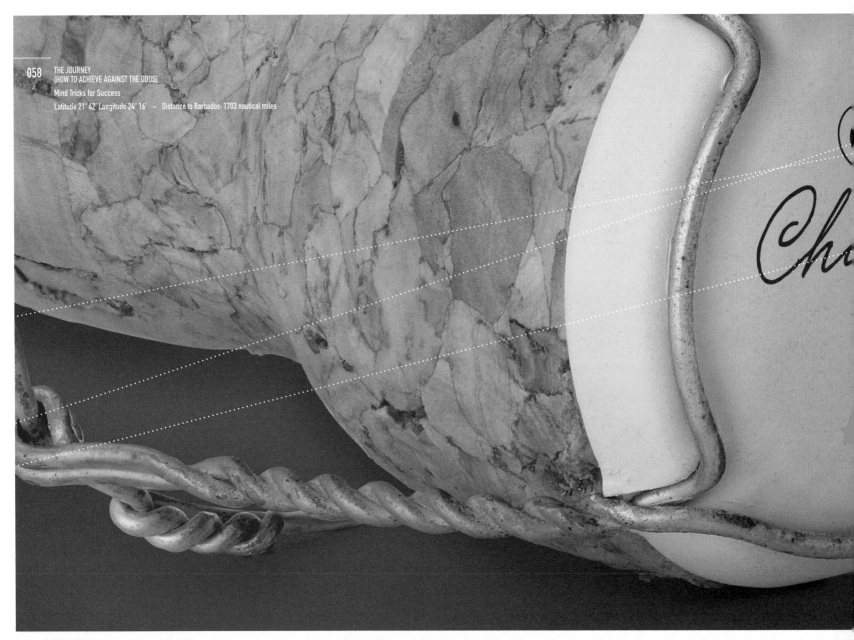

MIND TRICKS FOR
success

The 'Groundhog Day' feeling started to set in by the beginning of my second month at sea.

But the routine had to be there and I always stuck to the same routine. On waking up before my first row of the day I would switch on the GPS to check my position and how far I had been blown during my sleep period. On a good day I would have drifted towards Barbados 6 miles. On a bad day I would have been blown back 20 miles — the same 20 miles it had taken me the whole of the previous day to gain. Then I prepared for 'Row One'. I was always tired. During the first session back at the oars my body felt as if I had gone eight rounds in the ring with Lennox Lewis.

Probably the best way to describe it is by asking you to imagine yourself in a gym.

Take a seat on the rowing machine.

Programme two hours into the little display as the length of your training session.

Move the marker on the side of the flywheel to resistance setting 10 and press 'Start'.

Once you have completed the two hours you can get off the rowing machine for one hour but you have to stay within a radius of 1.5 metres of the rowing machine.

Fix and maintain the rowing machine.

Look at some navigation charts.

Go to the loo in a bucket.

Eat some food.

Sleep next to the machine on a piece of 5cm thick foam for however much time is remaining of the 60 minutes.

Get up and get back on the rowing seat.

Programme another two hours into the little display and off you go . . . again.

Repeat six times.

It is relentless!

However, there was much to find pleasure in. Sunrise was my favourite part of the day. I loved the way the shades of pinks and reds crept upwards, sending my 360-degree water world horizon into an excited glow. The water all around me would turn candyfloss pink and the light would bounce off it as if millions of diamonds were floating on the surface.

During breakfast, I would delight in the changing colours of the sky and the reflections on the water as I drank my hot chocolate, ate shortbread and breakfast bars. These moments of peace and tranquillity would occasionally cause me to cry tears of happiness. They were filled with such grace that I started to consider whether they were some kind of gift from God to rejuvenate me.

The breakfast rest period was also my main navigation time. I filled in the ships logbook with details of the weather and my position. The trade winds, which were supposed to be assisting my progress towards Barbados, had not yet arrived so my progress was painfully slow. To cover just a few millimetres on the Atlantic chart I would have to

'save up' totals from several days. By only plotting my position on the chart every five days I would get greatly encouraged by the illusion that I appeared to be moving. It became one of the many mind tricks for success that prevented me from getting totally demoralised by the snail-paced progress I was actually making.

It was depressing to roll out the whole chart in front of me and see the vast expanse of the ocean between my position, just off Africa, and Barbados on the other side. I soon learnt to trick my mind by rolling up the chart so that when I next pulled it out I would have to unroll it from the Africa side, only unrolling it as far as I had travelled. My focus was then on how far I had come rather than how far there was left to go to reach Barbados.

Achieving the goal of rowing single-handed to Barbados seemed a very long way away. I love setting myself big targets: the longest canoe race in the world, to sail round Antarctica, to make a BBC documentary, to write a book . . . but there is always that horribly hard bit when I question my sanity! This usually starts as soon as I allow myself to look at the overall picture, which inevitably I find completely overwhelming.

The above mind tricks helped me break it down into achievable sections, for which I always gave myself a reward. What's the point of achieving a big goal if there isn't a big, fat reward at the end of it? I pick something that I really want as a reward and attach it to an important goal so that I have something to motivate me onwards on the days when the mind tricks aren't working as effectively. Sometimes even those small goals that never seem to budge off my weekly to do list need a reward attached to them to make them happen. So I offer myself a coffee on Plymouth Hoe (one of my favourite places), provided the goal is achieved by lunch time. It usually works. It's just a shame that there wasn't more to reward myself with during my Atlantic crossing. It was hard to get motivated by the reward of another digestive biscuit!

In the daytime I always rowed naked, not because I'm a naturist or an exhibitionist but because it was the only way to prevent getting sores on my bottom.

Sitting on a small hard rowing seat in +30 degrees heat for twelve hours a day, covered in salt crystals and wearing shorts that caused sweating was a guaranteed way to get sores, boils or chafing on my bottom. With added infection, the pain of sitting on any surface, let alone a hard rowing seat, would be excruciating. This was something we had planned meticulously to avoid.

Andrew and I approached our boat builder and asked if he would take plaster casts of our bottoms — probably not a request he gets every day! From these he made fibreglass moulds to produce the perfectly fitted rowing seat. We then covered the seats in sheepskin. Letting the skin breathe and using the sheepskin seat covers was a definite 'bottom saver' but on the odd occasion when sores developed baby nappy rash cream certainly came to the rescue.

A new super fluffy, padded sheepskin seat cover was one of the most effective motivational rewards I had. When I reached another major line of longitude on my chart I celebrated by allowing myself a new sheepskin seat cover to sit on. Seat cover replacement brought my bottom much joy. If only all things in life could be so deeply satisfying!

Re-live a Moment

Latitude 18° 19′ Longitude 34° 07″   ~   Distance to Barbados: 1391 nautical miles

re-live
A MOMENT

Just before the end of November, after 7 weeks at sea, the satellite tracking system recorded that I was the second fastest boat in the fleet.

I thought 'Who needs two big strong guys in a boat when you can go faster with just one ickle me?'. I knew it was largely due to the front-runners being held up by hurricane Olga while I was surfing at speeds of up to 12 knots down some whopping great big waves. But I decided not to dwell on that minor detail!

During the same week I achieved a record breaking 43 nautical miles in 24 hours and had achieved similar distances on all the other days of that week. It felt as if I was finally being rewarded for my weeks of patience. Playing in the big surf everyday was awesome and I was completely in my element. I kept on thinking – surely I was born for this!

By the end of the first week in December I had reached the half way mark. Twenty out of the thirty-five crews that had started the Atlantic Rowing Race had finished. But I was unperturbed. Three crews had retired, resulting in two of the boats being scuttled. All three of the retired crews had first attempted to continue solo following their partner's rescues but they were unable to cope with the solitary lifestyle. It was down to me to prove it could be done.

It became incredibly exciting to plot my position on the chart at this time. For so long, it had looked as if I would never get away from the coast of Africa and the Cape Verde Islands. I had made such slow progress without the trade winds but now with more ocean behind me than in front, it became a real pleasure to spread the chart across the cabin and see how far I had come.

My ship's logbook only had 60 days worth of pages, as Andrew and I had hoped to finish in well under 60 days. Another notebook became logbook No. 2. I took the liberty of only writing in headings for days 61 to 100, as I set myself the goal of completing the challenge in less than 100 days. Christmas day would be day 80 with day 100 falling on Monday 14 January. It was going to be close, but I was focussed on a text message sent to my satellite phone describing perpetual optimism as a force multiplier. With so much time to think, I found myself deeply mulling over the quotes, bible verses and poems that people sent me, in a way I would not have done on any given day on dry land. They seemed to resonate with me and became a lifeline during times of adversity.

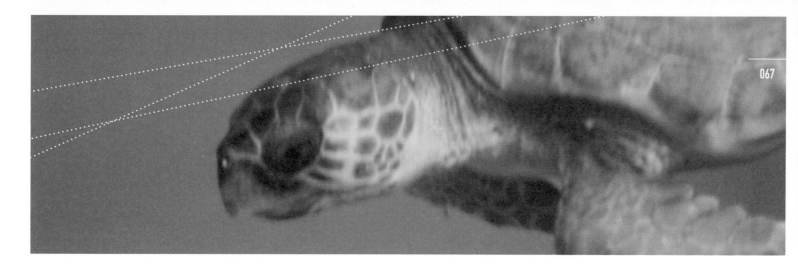

The loneliness was fast becoming my greatest challenge. Week after week of solitude left me desperately longing for someone to talk to face to face. There was no one even close. Consequently the wildlife around the boat received an outpouring of my love and attention, none more so than the sea turtles. They visited regularly and seemed completely at ease with my presence.

I decided that, out of all of the oceanic creatures I had observed, the sea turtles were definitely my favourite. The first sea turtle to visit I named Albert. No particular reason, he just looked like an Albert. I had never seen one up close before. I was surprised both by how Jurassic they were in appearance and how entertaining they were to watch. Albert seemed completely unbothered by me touching his shell but I made sure I kept my fingers away from his beak, which looked surprisingly vicious.

He must have thought all his Birthdays and Christmases had come at once, because not only had he found a boat with tasty fresh young weed growing on the hull but the boat also moved slow enough for him to keep up with it. I really was supplying a 'meals on hulls' service for my Jurassic friend. When he surfaced for air he exhaled, then inhaled with such gusto that his head wobbled and he went slightly cross-eyed. This reduced me to hysterical fits of giggles every time.

Albert also had a particular problem with diving back under the boat after he had come up for air. He repeatedly misjudged the manoeuvre and head butted the side of the boat resulting in more giggling than sympathy from me.

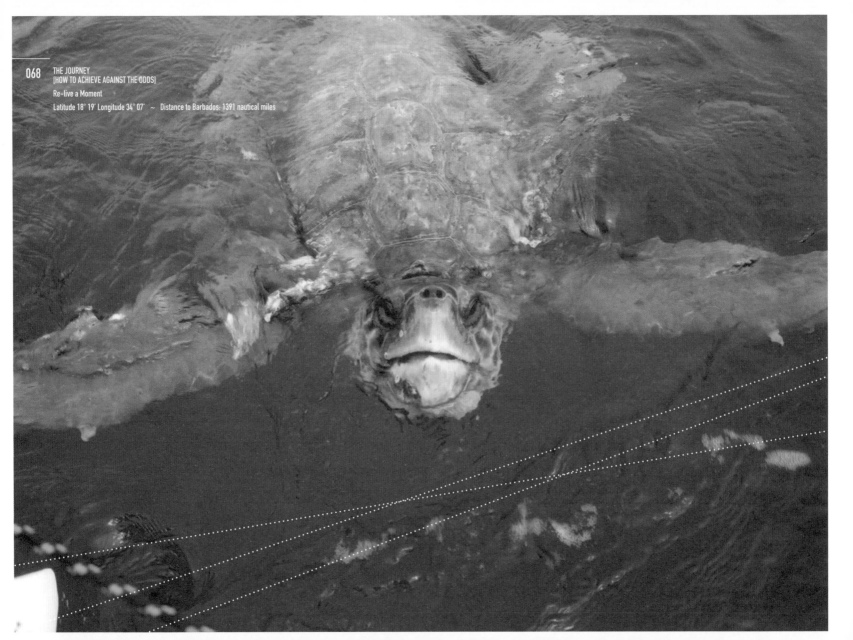

Conditions became rougher the nearer I got to the Caribbean due to the presence of two hurricanes just north of my position. One night the boat was being tossed around so much that objects were flying out of the storage pockets and hitting me as I tried to sleep. I was dozing when I heard a sound that I had not heard before. The waves and the wind were familiar after hearing almost nothing else for months, so any slight variation in sound would wake me in an instant. Now, a loud cracking noise was coming from the hull of the boat.

My heart racing, I peered through the water-splashed glass of the hatch, searching in the dark for the cause. My eyes immediately focused onto the portside oar. It was still in its gate, but instead of being in the usual horizontal storage position behind the frame on the bow it was sticking up vertically into the air.

The boat had turned sideways onto the waves and had washed the boat over the oar. The oar was about to snap, but the creaking noise from the pressure being exerted onto the plywood hull by the oar was far more of a concern. I had spare oars, but I couldn't magic up a spare hull.

The huge waves that forced Troika onto her side often only came along once in every set so there was no time to lose. If I didn't get the oar out from under the hull before the next big wave arrived I could lose an oar and have a hole in the hull to deal with. The prospect of sinking in these conditions was not a happy one. One big wave and I would be in serious trouble. Time-wise I felt I couldn't afford to struggle into my lifejacket and harness. I had to risk not being clipped in and hope that a 'big one' didn't hit while I was out on deck.

Once outside I made a dash for the oar, concentrating on keeping my centre of gravity low to absorb the force of the waves breaking up against the starboard side. I didn't even notice the waves soaking me as I pulled down on the handle end of the oar in an attempt to lever the blade end from under the hull. But the weight of the boat being pushed over the oar was too much and the blade was flat against the side. The resistance was too great. I knew I would have to twist the oar so that I could feather the blade out of the water. I didn't stand a chance otherwise.

I leaned over the side, trying to focus on the oar rather than the mass of aggressive foaming white water that was splashing up into my face. I felt fearless as I thrust my arm into the cold water.

At last, in between waves, the oar twisted. The blade cut through the water as easily as a hot knife through butter. But it was clear for only an instant, before it was ripped out of my hands and forced back into the water. As I got wetter I began to lose my purchase. Without my harness I could have so easily have slipped over the side. In my head I was saying 'Just stay calm Debs. You can do this. Just one more time and you'll soon be back in the cabin'.

With the same manoeuvre repeated, I was faster at storing the handle behind the frame the second time, and had it tied up as quick as lightning. I checked that the other oar was still secure and crawled towards the hatch. I looked to starboard at the barrage of oncoming waves. The white water bubbling at the crest of each wave glowed in the moonlight, highlighting the mighty power of the ocean. I waited for a smaller one then quickly opened the cabin hatch and dived in.

It was only when I was back in the cabin that I realised how foolish I had been to be out on deck in such conditions without a harness and lifejacket. The consequences of being washed overboard were far worse than having a crack in the hull. What was I thinking? My fearlessness and familiarity when working with the elements had blurred the edges of my own limitations and concern for personal safety. Having no fear had made me a danger to myself.

It's so easy to rush into something, full of determination and enthusiasm, only to realise afterwards just how foolish you have been. The aftermath requires me to fill my mind with something positive so that I don't spend the next hours, or sometimes days, chastising myself. A technique I often rely on is to re-live a moment of achievement or happiness.

I lay in the cabin that night, soaking wet, knowing I could ill-afford to start beating myself up over my stupidity so I forced myself to start re-living one of my most treasured memories. In an instant I was back in September 1998. Mum, Dad and Andrew travelled to Rome to watch me race at the European Championships with the Great Britain Dragon Boat squad. I had always wanted to represent my country in a sport, so it was a dream come true. Walking out in my Great Britain kit meant the world to me, and just as much to Mum and Dad. When I went up to collect my bronze and silver medals at the end of the Championships Dad was tearful with pride. I hadn't seen Mum and Dad looking so happy for ages. Dad's hair had just grown back after another course of chemotherapy and he looked really well. I took a photo of Mum and Dad just before I went up to collect my medals. The smiles on their faces said it all, and the pride in Dad's eyes that day is something I'll never forget.

That photo was stuck on the wall of the cabin for just such a moment. As I type it is now at eye level on the wall above my desk.

FREE
words

Every third day at sea I dictated my diary down the phone to Hayley.

She would use my diary to update my website and hand it to my shore team to email out to those who had asked to receive the newsletters. It initially went to friends and family but grew in popularity. Thousands of people from around the world began to sign up for it with anonymous helpers translating each diary update into their mother tongue and distributing my words in their country.

My webmaster Leigh found a way for supporters to text my satellite phone via the Inmarsat website and he asked people to send words of encouragement. The response was phenomenal. Hundreds of people sent encouraging messages:

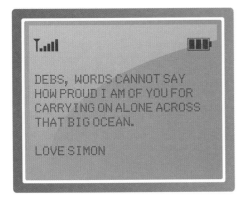

DEBS, WORDS CANNOT SAY HOW PROUD I AM OF YOU FOR CARRYING ON ALONE ACROSS THAT BIG OCEAN.

LOVE SIMON

HI DEBS JUST HEARD ABOUT ANDREW — GLAD TO HEAR YOU'RE STILL GOING FOR IT — ATTAGIRL! BEST WISHES,

MARTIN WARD

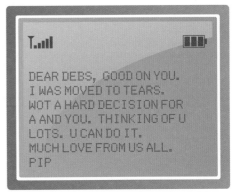

DEAR DEBS, GOOD ON YOU. I WAS MOVED TO TEARS. WOT A HARD DECISION FOR A AND YOU. THINKING OF U LOTS. U CAN DO IT. MUCH LOVE FROM US ALL. PIP

KEEP AT IT GIRL! MY UTMOST
RESPECT FOR GOING IT
ALONE. I FLEW BACK FROM
U. S. YESTERDAY & THOUGHT
OF YOU DOWN THERE IN THE
DARK SOMEWHERE.
LIZ (TWRC)

The text messages became a huge part of my journey. At the start of every rest period I would switch on the satellite phone desperately hoping to receive some text messages. It was always a real disappointment to get none. It left me feeling alone and stranded. Fortunately this rarely happened. More often than not I would receive messages that would either have me crying with laughter, humbled or feeling supported and cared for. The strange thing was that the text messages, even the personal ones from my close family members and friends, never made me feel homesick. They were the reassurance I needed.

After two months alone I hit an all time emotional low and became reliant on the text message more than ever. All of those strategies I had been relying on to keep me motivated seemed to gradually loose their impact as the loneliness riddled my mind and body. I longed to have physical contact with someone . . . anyone.

The loneliness was all consuming. The realisation that I was not going to make it to Barbados to be with my family for Christmas completely crushed me and started to affect me in dramatic ways. My body began to reject all food and water. I struggled to drink 1 litre of water a day when I should have been drinking 8–10. Consequently I felt weak, and rowing seemed harder than ever. I just couldn't fight with the waves in such a condition and constantly dissolved in tears whilst sitting at the oars. Every minor task seemed like a major challenge and caused even more bottom-lip trembling. I felt as if I was losing the will to live.

I forced myself to write a diary entry, but couldn't face trying to make it sound like everything was peachy and I was having a fab time. To avoid worrying my family I had always tried to sound positive in my diary updates, but I didn't have the energy anymore. I hated the idea of showing my vulnerability to the team back home but I had no choice. For the first time my diary contained the absolute truth. I shared the unbearable loneliness and told them that all I wanted for Christmas was a hug.

Within hours of this diary entry being posted on the Troika Transatlantic website I was inundated with supportive text messages from around the globe and become the proud owner of more virtual hugs than anyone else in the world! Without this support from the world outside of my little rowing boat I am not sure I would have made it.

Crazy isn't it . . . we struggle to communicate with the person who sits at the desk next to us and yet just one text message can empower someone to achieve in the face of great adversity. I'm always mindful that if that is what a text message can do then just think what a face to face meeting can achieve. It's given me a desire to give up on faceless emailing and it has encouraged me to meet people in person. Hayley and I now have a rule at work: 'always take the meeting'.

Free Words

Latitude 16° 20' Longitude 41° 56' ~ Distance to Barbados: 997 nautical miles

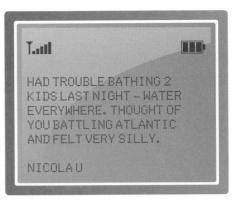

HAD TROUBLE BATHING 2
KIDS LAST NIGHT – WATER
EVERYWHERE. THOUGHT OF
YOU BATTLING ATLANTIC
AND FELT VERY SILLY.

NICOLA U

MORNING, JO HERE.
WEIRD EXPERIENCE TODAY.
MET SOMEONE IN A MEETING
WHO I NEVER MET BEFORE.
I MENTIONED I ROWED.
HE SAID HAVE YOU HEARD OF
THAT AMAZING WOMAN WHO
IS ROWING THE ATLANTIC
SINGLE–HANDED.

THATS YOU D!

IT WAS WONDERFUL TO HEAR
THE IMPRESSION U ARE
MAKING ON PEOPLE YOU
HAVE NEVER MET.
L. O. L, JO XX

EXPRESS DELIVERY FOR
DEBRA. AN UNFEASIBLY LARGE
AND EXTREMELY HUGGY HUG.
WITH LOTS OF LOVE *H.

OH GO ON HAVE ANOTHER
ONE THEN!

HI DEB. GOT A COLD, FEELING
BLUE, READ YOUR DIARY PAGE
– INSPIRED AT LAST – WORK TO
DO! KEEP UP THE GOOD WORK!

LOVE DEB WARD

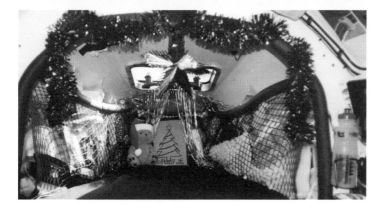

Not surprisingly, I had more responses from that diary update than any other. It was a real lesson to me that it is perfectly fine to show your vulnerability and ask for extra help from the team back home, even when you are meant to be leading it, as it empowers them and calls them to action.

My phone could only hold 30 messages, so each time I cleared the inbox it filled up straight away with another 30! The words were so encouraging and what blew my mind was that they were free. It cost those people nothing to say them.

I thought a great deal about the power of free words while I was at sea (I had an awful lot of time to think!) and the fact that our supply of free words is unlimited. With them we have the power to uplift or destroy someone's confidence and that choice is ours. Sometimes I lay in bed at night and think, 'who have I encouraged today and how well did I use my free words?'. Some days I realise I haven't said anything positive to anyone all day. By choosing to use my free words positively, to uplift others a little more than I used to, I have noticed a dramatic difference in the results I have achieved, both with clients and colleagues. It has got to be worth a try. After all, it doesn't cost anything.

With a little help from my friends, most of whom I will never meet, I had been lifted from the depths of loneliness and was on a roll again. Deep down I knew I had already come too far to give up. Patience was what I needed and if I could find it I would soon know the most overwhelming sense of achievement, which could never be taken away from me. It would be an achievement that would make all the days of loneliness worth it.

The team didn't stop there in their drive to keep me going and endlessly sought ways to encourage me. To get around my growing disappointment that I was going to have to spend Christmas Day alone at sea they arranged for me to have the most unique Christmas ever, to make up for the fact that I couldn't be at home with them. I had been disqualified from the race when Andrew left the boat as I was deemed to have accepted outside assistance, so the team used this unfortunate circumstance to their advantage and arranged for a parcel drop. The parcel drop was only allowed because, officially, I was no longer in the race.

Ten days before Christmas I watched the mast light of the support yacht slowly getting brighter. As they sailed towards me I got increasingly excited about seeing people again for the first time in months. The crew launched a dinghy and Gavin and John, two crewmembers, rowed over with two big bin liners of food and Christmas presents for me. I couldn't believe it! The team back home had excelled themselves. John and Gavin kindly hung on to the side of Troika Transatlantic for ten minutes so that we could have a face-to-face chat, which was wonderful. When the time came for them to row back to the yacht I wanted to give each of them a big hug, but I guess I was a bit out of practice at socialising and felt too embarrassed. I was really sad to see them go.

Hayley had enclosed some Christmas decorations for the boat in my parcel and my brother Matt had included a tiny Christmas pudding. The plan was coming together nicely for the most unique Christmas ever! The only thing missing was some turkey. A chicken-flavoured Cup-a-Soup would have to suffice!

She also enclosed a book called 'What's So Amazing About Grace' by Philip Yancey. Having only had one book on board which I had read three times already I was very excited to have some new reading material, but it turned out to be more life changing than entertaining. It challenged every stereotype and frustration I had of the Christian Church in the West and really got me thinking . . . yet again more thinking!

Later, as I watched their sails disappearing over the horizon, already feeling emotional because of everyone's kindness, Troika was suddenly surrounded by dolphins, maybe as many as thirty. It was as if they had been sent to console me with their company, to stop me getting sad that I was alone again. I tried to count them but they moved too fast. Their movements were enormously playful and they seemed to have constant grins on their faces. Two of them even leapt out of the water and completed front flips, landing with big splashes. To watch this real life entertainment in the wild was breathtaking and completely overwhelming. I stood there with the biggest smile on my face, crying tears of happiness, feeling like the luckiest person alive and thanking God for the beauty of his remarkable creation. For the first time ever I was able to make that link and believe it to be true. Surely God is behind all this because it is just too beautiful for it to be chance.

The Easy Option is Never the Most Rewarding

Latitude 13° 41′ Longitude 52° 49′   ~   Distance to Barbados: 221 nautical miles

THE EASY OPTION
IS NEVER THE
most
rewarding

Some nights in my final weeks at sea, the sky was at bursting point with stars.

I knew I would not see starry skies like them back in urban England. The sunrise each morning was as soothing as ever after a violent night of wave wrestling. In my fragile state, I needed its touch. Week after week of twelve hours a day, solitary hard labour was taking its toll. My body was screaming for some normality — a rest from rowing, a still bed, a toilet with a seat, regular showers and some fresh food — the things most of us generally take for granted.

My emotions were taking a roller-coaster ride. One hour I was desperate for it to all be over, the next I was content not wanting it to end. Lack of sleep during those rough nights meant I overreacted to almost everything. My ability to cope seemed to dissolve. Every day felt like a lifetime. My highs were staying around for shorter periods while my lows were lingering, and that wasn't good. I had to reach Barbados before the lows started to outnumber the highs. Yet, I didn't want to wish away what I had out there. It was an extraordinary experience, shared by only a few. Deep down I knew I was extremely fortunate. I just had to remind myself of that during the tough times.

I believe that a negative situation can nearly always be turned into a positive one and, if nothing else, there is always the scope to learn. Receiving a text from my good friend Mike Barker allowed me to see how. "I think despair comes just before enlightenment" he said, and he was right. When we are stripped bare, metaphorically speaking, and are at our lowest ebb, we have the opportunity to discover ourselves.

Whether we choose to take that opportunity is another matter.

The last few weeks of the journey gave me that opportunity - and more time to explore it than most - learning an enormous amount about myself and what I was capable of achieving. I was further outside my comfort zone than I had been at any other point during the voyage but it was only by being pushed to these outer limits that I discovered how strong my mind was. I realise now how often I may have chosen the easy option in the past, either because I wasn't aware of my mental strength or feared failure. We all choose the easy option from time to time if we're honest but I now know that taking the easy option is never the most rewarding and can ultimately leave us unfulfilled.

The only way that I was going to get to Barbados quicker was if I spent more time at the oars. I had started to drop to ten hours rowing a day and sometimes only managed eight, when Hayley sent me a message:

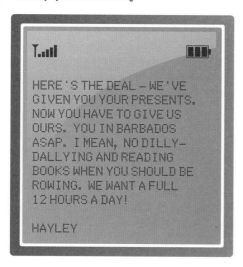

HERE'S THE DEAL — WE'VE GIVEN YOU YOUR PRESENTS. NOW YOU HAVE TO GIVE US OURS. YOU IN BARBADOS ASAP. I MEAN, NO DILLY-DALLYING AND READING BOOKS WHEN YOU SHOULD BE ROWING. WE WANT A FULL 12 HOURS A DAY!

HAYLEY

My brother Matt then replied with:

DEBS — MATT HERE. DON'T LISTEN TO HAYLEY — ROW SLOWER. THE AIR FARES GET CHEAPER IN FEBRUARY!

To keep my promise to Hayley (and ignoring Matt's humour) I had stern words with myself and started a full 12 hours a day at the oars, storms permitting. I even started adding an extra 15 minutes to my rowing shifts here and there, if I could manage it. But I was so exhausted. Often I would catch myself sitting at the oars motionless, staring vacantly. Or I would just sit there and cry. In those moments of desperation I would snap myself out of it by saying, "Come on Debra, this isn't going to get you there. Start running the movie". The movie was always the same and I watched it in my head hundreds of times.

It was of my landfall moment.

It was the only thing that could keep me pulling the oars through the water because I wanted that moment to happen more than I had ever wanted anything else in my life. I could spend a good hour working through the whole scene – colours, sounds, smells, seeing my family on the shore, what I would say to them, what they might say to me, how I would feel, and so on. How I longed for that moment.

Reaching day 100 felt like a huge achievement. I had known for weeks that I wasn't going to make Barbados in less than 100 days and accepted that, as hard as I might try, I could not change the weather. I had to travel at whatever speed the elements dictated. Reaching day 100 gave me a perfect time to reflect. To mark that special centenary day I wanted to summarise the highs and the lows, the weird and the wonderful of 100 days in my water-world, so I spent a few enjoyable and enlightening rest periods reading back through my diary and log book to compile a series of 'Top Tens' of my voyage to include on the website. The strongest impression, as I turned the pages was just how far I had come, not only in nautical miles, but also mentally, emotionally and spiritually. Being alone at sea had made me learn and grow in ways that might not have been possible had Andrew stayed on board. Perhaps reluctantly, I had to believe that for that reason alone my solo journey was meant to be.

It increasingly looked as if my return to the real world was going to be a hectic one. I had been told to expect a number of journalists, photographers and film crews when I arrived in Barbados, and was more than a bit concerned about the transition from total isolation to a hive of social activity and media interest. Every time I thought about it, I reminded myself of part of a quote I was sent: " . . .no matter what happens, never act out of character."

Defining my character in a way that would help me never to act outside of it was something that Hayley pushed very hard for when we launched a business together. In a role that is heavily client and media facing she constantly impressed on me the importance of having a personal set of brand values to stand by and to set me apart from my competitors. We defined them together and she made me promise that I would never do anything to contradict these values. I have six. They are hardworking, honest, family-orientated, adventurous, feminine and fun-loving. In everything I do I try to exude these values. Even when I am outside my comfort zone and working on something new I focus hard on maintaining these brand values. It is the one thing that has to remain consistent particularly when projects or the market is changing rapidly. I have also found it very helpful when working with the media.

By day 111 at sea the chart was telling me that I was about to bump into Barbados but could I see it! Other crews had told me that they had been able to see Barbados with around 25 miles to go. I eagerly anticipated that first satisfying glimpse. But as the day stretched on, I still couldn't see the island. I wasn't worried as I felt confident in my navigation and knew it was out there somewhere. I needed that glimpse for satisfaction more than anything else, so every few strokes I would look over my shoulder, scanning the horizon. But all I could see was a bank of cloud. Cloud shapes kept teasing, convincing me that they were Barbados, as I didn't really know what it would look like. I wasn't sure if I was looking for a pimple on the horizon or a long, flat slice of land.

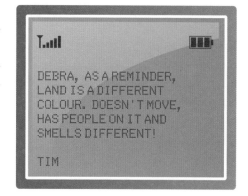

DEBRA, AS A REMINDER, LAND IS A DIFFERENT COLOUR. DOESN'T MOVE, HAS PEOPLE ON IT AND SMELLS DIFFERENT!

TIM

088 THE JOURNEY
[HOW TO ACHIEVE AGAINST THE ODDS]
The Easy Option is Never the Most Rewarding
Latitude 13° 41´ Longitude 52° 49´ ~ Distance to Barbados: 221 nautical miles

At sunset my waiting was over. As the sun shone through the bank of cloud a silhouette of the island seemed to appear from nowhere and suddenly looked as if it was right next to me — a surprisingly long, flat, slice. As darkness fell I was left gazing at Barbados, the lights a glittering prize set in front of me.

I really was going to make it.

Yet, instead of being elated I began to feel uncomfortable. Frightened even. I realised I was scared of returning to dry land. Of being part of a crowd; of the sights and sounds to which I'd grown unaccustomed; the demands and routine of 'society.'

I had become so used to my solitary world on the beautiful ocean in Troika: the constant motion and natural sounds; being hit by flying fish and chased by turtles; my two-hours-on, one-hour-off routine; not wearing any clothes and not having to care, and most importantly not having anyone around whose opinion I felt I had to live up to.

I had grown completely accustomed to life onboard. It was what I knew best. I understood how to respond to the boat and the conditions, but life on land had become alien to me. I had loved living in a world filled with grace and was concerned about returning to a dog-eat-dog society.

Exhaustion set in but I didn't want to fall asleep on the last night and drift onto the rocks. I knew that the most hazardous part of any ocean crossing was the start and finish when there is land about. I was too excited and nervous to sleep anyway. I was due to cross the finish line at approximately 5am. Andrew and I had discussed the option of the family all coming out on boats to be at the line of longitude that would be my finish, but the conditions were appalling. It would not have been safe, and I would be crossing the finishing line in the dark - not great for spectators.

Things were about to go crazy on the media front. Little did I know that The Times newspaper had hit the newsstands with a large picture of me on the front page. It was still 2am local time for me, but 6am in England. Breakfast television shows had just started and a review of the papers exposed my story. A text message soon arrived from BBC Breakfast News asking if I was prepared to do a live phone interview.

As I was up anyway I thought I might as well. I quite liked the idea of having a practice interview before reaching the journalists on land. What I didn't realise was that all TV and radio news programmes watch and listen to each other. As soon as I had finished the BBC interview, I was bombarded with phone calls and text messages asking for more. It all seemed very surreal!

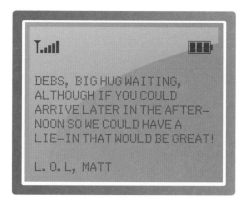

DEBS, BIG HUG WAITING, ALTHOUGH IF YOU COULD ARRIVE LATER IN THE AFTER- NOON SO WE COULD HAVE A LIE-IN THAT WOULD BE GREAT!

L. O. L, MATT

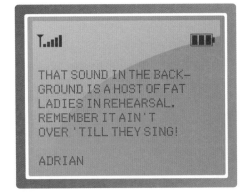

THAT SOUND IN THE BACK-
GROUND IS A HOST OF FAT
LADIES IN REHEARSAL.
REMEMBER IT AIN'T
OVER 'TILL THEY SING!

ADRIAN

As the morning drew on I rounded the northern tip of Barbados in very rough conditions. One by one boats carrying well wishers started to arrive. Barbadians had embraced my story and the whole island knew about the mad British girl who had been at sea alone for over three months. More and more boats surrounded me as we approached Port St Charles, accompanied by shouting and horn blowing. Two kayakers joined me. They must have come miles to greet me. I couldn't believe that so many people had come to see me in, despite the rain and choppy conditions. The atmosphere was amazing. Far from feeling nervous with so many people, as I'd expected, their smiling faces and warm welcome started to make me feel at ease.

I was desperate to get to my family waiting at the port so was completely flabbergasted to spot a speed boat crammed full of familiar looking blue Troika team uniforms hurtling towards me. Unable to wait any longer, they had persuaded a local resident of Port St Charles to give them a lift out to see me in. Suddenly the most important boat of all was right next to me. The look of pride on my mother's face made me somehow instantly forget all of the terrifying nights, the stormy seas and the days of desperate loneliness. It made me smile to think that if Dad had lived long enough to share this moment he probably would have been stood next to Mum in floods of tears — he was such a lovely, big softy.

092   THE JOURNEY
       [HOW TO ACHIEVE AGAINST THE ODDS]
       The Easy Option is Never the Most Rewarding
       Latitude 13° 41' Longitude 52° 49' ~ Distance to Barbados: 221 nautical miles

Dad had been such a source of inspiration throughout the journey. He had been having chemotherapy for the best part of four years before he died. He never once complained and his joyous, bubbly nature was totally contagious to the nurses and all of us around him. This time alone at sea had finally made me accept that I could let go of him without forgetting him; that I could remember his enthusiasm, his eternal optimism and his love of life – and emulate it.

My family and the team had such massive smiles on their faces. They had every right to smile and celebrate. I couldn't have made it without them. This was their moment too. They choose to mark it with a tongue in cheek banner in the form of a huge sheet which they held up on the bow of the boat. It read "COME IN No.22 YOUR TIME IS UP". They were right. My time was most definitely up. It was time to bring this awesome adventure to a close.

WARD EVANS
CHALLENGE
www.wardevans.com
22
troika transatlantic
WARD EVANS
Partners in Intelligent Solutions
www.wardevans.com
art
well hung a

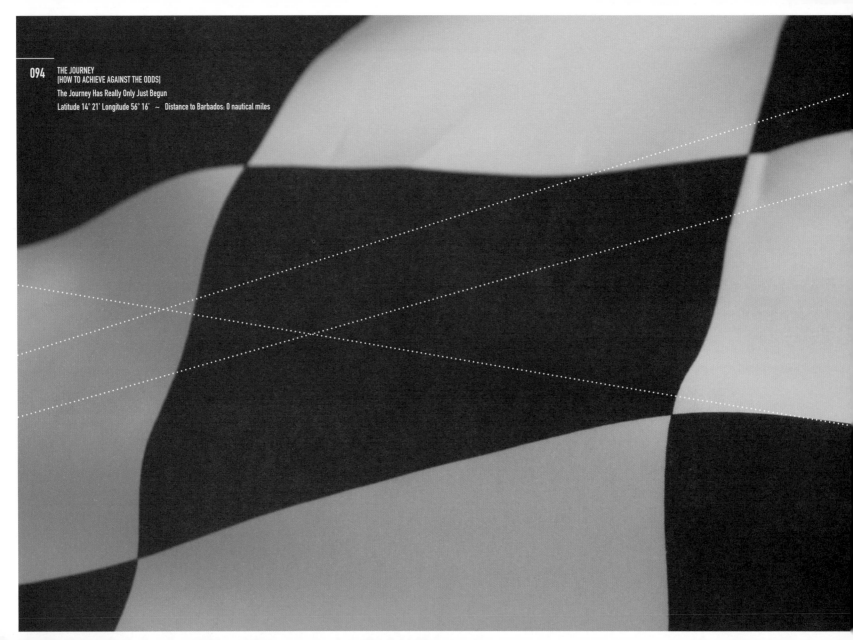

The Journey Has Really Only Just Begun

Latitude 14° 21' Longitude 56° 16' ~ Distance to Barbados: 0 nautical miles

THE JOURNEY HAS REALLY only just begun

I was the last boat to cross the finish line.

I didn't mind being last at all. I was so determined to win the race before we left Tenerife but looking back I realise that determination left me on night one, when I first glimpsed Andrew's fear. By day two I knew the experience was going to be vastly different from the one we had set out to have. The race no longer mattered.

During that first week at sea, over 100 days ago, our sole focus had been to do everything we could to stick to the original plan — to row across the Atlantic together. But things didn't always go according to plan. After Andrew was rescued, winning and proving all my doubters wrong became totally unimportant. I wonder now whether it ever really mattered. It ceased being about records or marking my place in history. It became 100% about the journey and what I learnt and experienced along the way. I learnt so very much but perhaps the most important lesson was this — things don't have to go to plan to work out well.

As I rowed towards the entrance to Port St Charles I could see hundreds of people lining the helipad on the quayside. Boats were coming right up with congratulations.

DEBRA, YOU'VE BEEN IN THAT BOAT NEARLY HALF MY LIFE!

LOVE TILLY MASON
AGED 7½ MONTHS

I was still fifty metres from land, but already microphones were being thrust in my face. Photographers were hanging from small speedboats, shouting.

"Debra! Debra! This way! This way!"
"Look like you're really pulling hard!"

I was pulling hard. I had no option other than to pull hard, as I was going nowhere fast in a head wind. Each stroke felt as if I was rowing into a brick wall, and I was getting redder in the face with the exertion.

Everyone was cheering and blowing horns, but my excitement was draining somewhat. My frustration built as the wind tried to prevent me covering those final metres. Clearly, rowing the Atlantic was going to be hard until the very end. I was reminded of a phrase painted on the side of Bright Spark, another competitor's boat.

It read "NOTHING GREAT IS EASY".

I started driving with my legs as hard as I could. I was barely moving, only just creeping forwards, willing myself with each stroke. As I approached the helipad I was more sheltered from the wind and rowing started to get a bit easier. The boat picked up speed and at last I was getting there.

The atmosphere was electric. The crowd cheered. I could feel every one of them willing me on.

As I drew parallel with the helipad I jumped off my seat and grabbed a spare oar that was lying on the deck next to me. This was my opportunity to give a victory salute and I felt I had earned the right to take it. I lifted it above my head and a deafening cheer erupted. The crowd went wild and boats everywhere blew their horns raucously.

The Journey Has Really Only Just Begun

Latitude 14° 21' Longitude 56° 16' ~ Distance to Barbados: 0 nautical miles

My senses suddenly kicked in, released by the relief of arrival. Each one competed with another, sharpening my experience. The scent of the crowd and the land was heady. The vibrant colours, after shades of only blue and grey for month, were almost startling. But the incredible noise won easily. I still had to row around the pontoon, under the bow of a 120-foot super-yacht. It sounded its horn and I could feel the noise vibrating in my lungs. Every one of my senses was so sharp. It was like being reborn and experiencing each one for the first time.

As I rounded the super-yachts, I could see Andrew and Sir Chay Blyth waiting for me. I was so eager to get to Andrew that I wasn't really concentrating on steering the boat and almost rammed the pontoon! But there were others ready to pull Troika Transatlantic in.

As I came alongside, Sir Chay let loose with a bottle of champagne and hit the bull's eye. As I wiped the champagne from my eyes Andrew was right there in front of me. He reached down into the boat and put his arms around me to give me a huge hug.

"You made it!" were Andrew's first words to me.

Attempting to walk on dry land was hilarious. My calf muscles had wasted away, and my ability to balance had gone with them. It really was the strangest sensation. I just couldn't stand up if I wasn't holding onto someone or something. Even then, I would be fine one minute then on the floor the next after my knees had buckled and my calves could not rectify the situation. I wobbled and swayed my way into the customs building on the shoulder of Teresa, the race manager, as Andrew was not allowed into customs with me.

I had to go through customs before I was allowed to see the rest of my family. The office was air-conditioned, the mood serious and quiet. I sat down to sign some papers but was on such a high at being around people I knew, that all I wanted to do was talk. And talk I did — incessantly.

I was so excited that I couldn't concentrate and the customs officers weren't very amused! They repeatedly put papers in front of me with the instruction, "Sign and date please".

Each time I couldn't remember how to sign my name and kept forgetting the date. I shivered from the air-conditioning, having not experienced cold air for four months, but nothing could chill the warm grin on my face. The stamp the customs officer thumped onto my passport seemed to seal my arrival and top my excitement for it read, "Barbados – Entry by Sea". Brilliant!

I had known the ultimate adventure. I had seen awesome wildlife, survived more than enough scary moments and had done an enormous amount of soul searching, but nothing could beat the intensity of the feeling of achievement that I felt at that moment.

My relief at not having to spend every moment of every day battling to survive in such a hostile place was tangible.
The feeling of satisfaction amazing.
My happiness complete.
I had done it.
I had rowed the Atlantic Ocean – for Dad, for my family, for Andrew and for me.
I had dared to believe and my dream had come true.
I felt so ALIVE!

It was, indeed, good to have an end to the journey . . . but it was the journey that mattered in the end.

Top ten worst memories:

10. The day I had beef stew and dumplings for the fifth day in a row.

9. Day 93 — When I woke to find almost 40 dead flying fish on the boat. I normally only found about 10 at the most. The stench was overpowering and they left every surface covered in fish scales and slime.

8. Day 91 — Splash-back from the poo-bucket. As I threw the contents overboard it splashed back into my face and into my mouth. Much spitting and rubbing with baby wet wipes followed.

7. Night of Day 89 — One of the roughest nights. At 4am an oar broke free whilst still in its gate, but wrapped itself under the boat. Fighting with the oar as the waves broke over me was not a good night out!

6. Day 85 (between Christmas and New Year) — In my diary I wrote, "I feel so worn down. Every time I look out of the hatch at the ocean I feel so trapped because I know I can't give up.". I got myself so worked up about having to spend another four weeks alone that I was inconsolable for much of the afternoon.

5. Day 19 — A shark swam under the boat that night, chasing fish. I watched the trail of glowing phosphorescence as it shot through the water at high speeds and convinced myself that it was going to attack the boat. I hid in the cabin, very scared until dawn.

4. Day 14 — The day Andrew left the boat. As I watched the yacht sail towards us on its way to pick up Andrew we held each other and cried. I couldn't help thinking that if anything went wrong we might never see each other again.

3. Ten days of unbearable loneliness at the start of December, which climaxed on day 65 when I cried from 8am till 11am, when I finally found enough strength to get out of the cabin and row. My diary that day read, "...wind was so strong, fighting the waves kept on making me dissolve into tears. I'm so exhausted and just want to sleep".

2. Day 23 — Everything seemed to be going wrong, then I nearly got run down by a super tanker. I wrote in my diary, "I am at an all time low and don't know if I am going to be able to recover . . . I'm so scared and I want to go home".

1. Day 8 — Disastrous day for a very unhappy Andrew. It culminated in a thunder and lightning storm with driving rain and, having completed a double night shift, I found Andrew in the cabin curled up, shaking and unable to even talk to me.

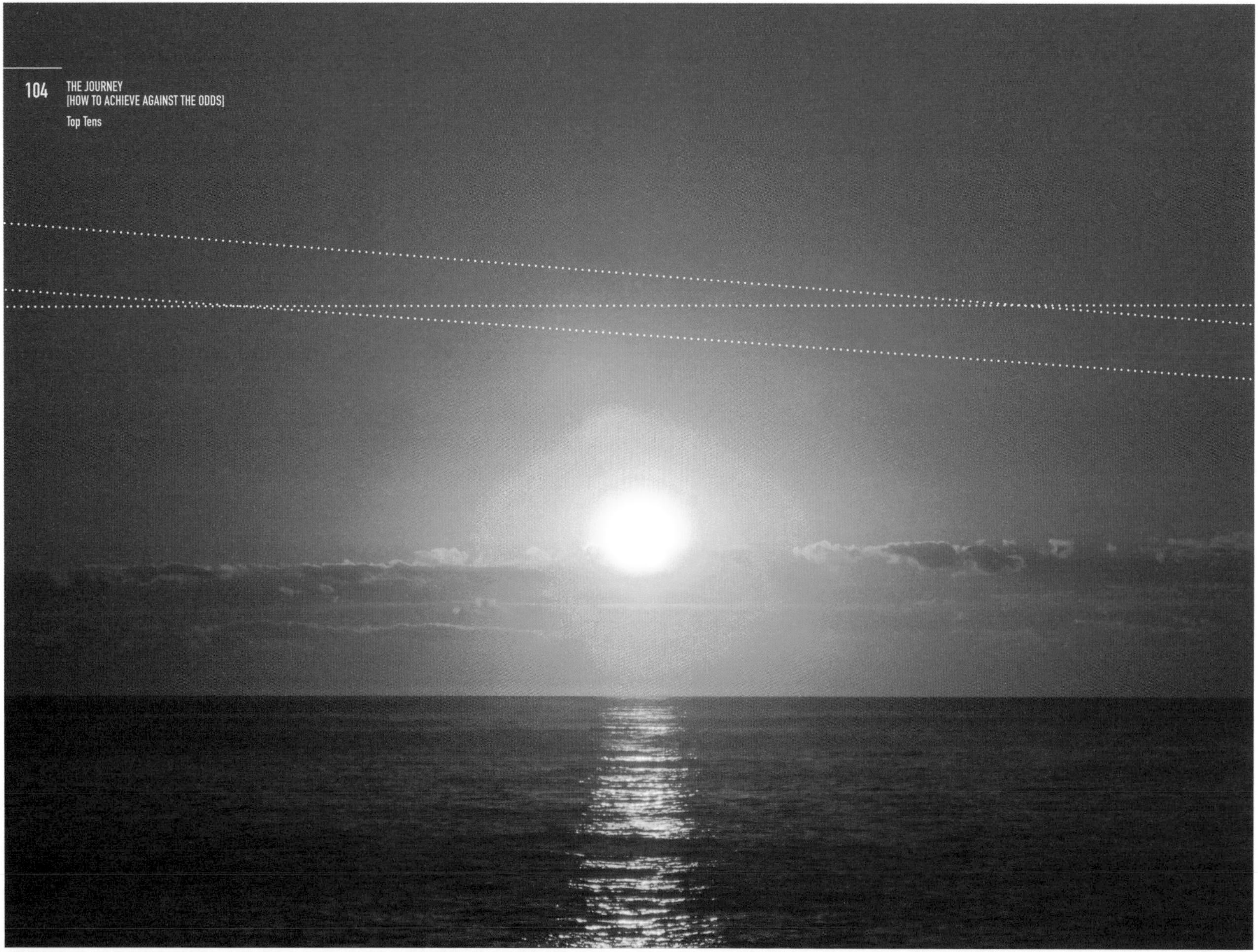

Top ten best memories:

10. Day 6 – First night rowing with the stars out. It was breathtakingly beautiful as I watched dozens of shooting stars trailing across the night sky.

9. Day 64 – After an emotional day crying at the oars, I was looking for the rice and found a whole bag of thirty Pepperamis and thirty packs of Minstrels that I had forgotten.

8. Day 74 – Having not seen anyone for a month, I crossed sea-paths with a yacht called 'Seventh Heaven' whose crew gave me a loaf of fresh bread, some awesome chocolate biscuits and, more importantly, ten minutes of talking face to face with 'other humans'.

7. Day 76 – Secretly arranged to talk via speakerphone to all the Troika staff while they were in a company meeting just before Christmas. It was a great surprise – they all cheered like mad.

6. Day 54 – First day of surfing really big waves. I wrote in my diary, "It was awesome – I LOVE IT!". That evening my face ached from grinning so much.

5. Day 24 – The day I spent with Albert the turtle while he ate weed off the hull. I had never seen a sea turtle up close before and was even able to touch him – fantastic.

4. Day 75 – Having enjoyed a visit from the Challenge yacht who brought me my Christmas parcel, the boat was then surrounded by 30 dolphins, two of whom did front somersaults right in front of me. It was truly magical to see this in the wild.

3. Christmas Day – Reading all my Christmas cards from my friends and family in the UK.

2. Day 4 – Rowing at 3am with Andrew, singing "Jerusalem" and "I Vow to Thee My Country" at the top of our voices to keep ourselves awake, and laughing at Andrew's flexible approach to musicality!

1. Day 21 – Watching the most beautiful sunrise, I felt all the pain and anguish over my father's premature death fade away leaving me crying tears of happiness. I came to a point where I could celebrate his life and take inspiration from it, rather than dwell on my loss.

THE TIMES
Monday January 28 ~ Leading Article

QUEEN OF THE HIGH SEAS
A transatlantic heroine makes landfall

A low moan stole across the waters of the Atlantic last night. The Nereids sighed and drooped their lovely heads – not since Thetis's departure had they lost such a sister. Poseidon lolled wretchedly about his kingdom, wistfully caressing his beard. Not since his tussle with Athene had he relished such a contest. His horses tossed their manes. Where would they find such a racing companion? Only Amphitrite looked relieved, arms folded, eyeing the Barbados shoreline and a touching reunion between husband and wife. Hasn't she had enough problems with mermaids over the years without the addition of a golden-haired human speeding naked across the waves? After 112 days watching a love affair between a mortal and the deep, there was one place she wanted Ms Debra Veal and that was back on land.

She got her wish. The Ward Evans Atlantic Rowing Challenge is over, and the winner is the contestant who came last. After more than three months at sea, Debra Veal – businesswoman, maritime nudist and consumer of more beef stew than a human should have to face – was lifted out of her craft by the husband who abandoned her to a lone quest. Onlookers went wild, tears and champagne flowed, and our heroine found that sea legs would not so easily convert into landlubber limbs. And unlike the chaps who preceded her, Ms Veal turned up looking spick and span with clean hair and outfit and a very impressive tan.

Also unlike the chaps she did it alone. Ward Evans competitors were supposed to row in pairs but not everyone could take the pressure of the open seas, Ms Veal's husband included. While other deserted partners, including Times man Jonathan Gornall, eventually renounced the solo quest, Debs rowed on with the indomitable spirit shown by the little red hen in the children's fairy tale. The men got angsty and existential. Ms Veal was in her element — row, row, rowing her boat gently 'cross the stream, bumping into turtles and laughing gaily whilst being slapped in the face by flying fish. Like the yachtswoman Ellen MacArthur, Ms Veal's Journey was spiritual as much as physical, a stripping away of layers until she reached her self's inner core, an achievement that she describes as a state of grace.

No one knows what they will find when they set out on such an adventure, but Ms Veal has come away with the ultimate reward. Armchair mariners everywhere can draw inspiration from her voyage of self-discovery. As she toasted her boat, Troika Transatlantic, 'this lady, this very special lady', so we, in turn, salute her.

About the Author

Debra Searle MBE MA is a truly inspirational woman. Debra confounded the sceptics by rowing single-handedly across the Atlantic, after her husband and team-mate was forced to retire suffering from an uncontrollable fear of the ocean.

Despite a poor performance at school she found a way to tap into her potential and graduated from university with 1st Class Honours, founded her first company at the age of 24 and her second at 27. Debra is an author of and contributor to three books and has represented Great Britain at European and World Championship level.

Debra is a regular presenter for the BBC, with credits including Grandstand, Extreme Lives, and Builders, Sweat and Tears. Her spirit of adventure gained Debra an MBE from Her Majesty the Queen and she was delighted to be invited to join the board of trustees of the Duke of Edinburgh's Award in 2003, the youngest and only female trustee working alongside His Royal Highness The Duke of Edinburgh and His Royal Highness The Earl of Wessex.

Debra is an experienced and dedicated motivational speaker working with some of the largest companies in the world. She is not a speaker reliant on buzz words, hype and jargon but uses her stories to subtly draw out key business and personal lessons.

Debra's recent expeditions have included sailing around Antarctica and becoming the first Briton to complete the grueling Yukon River Quest — the longest canoe race in the world.

She grew up on the edge of Dartmoor in Devon, England with her two older brothers and her identical twin sister. She has remarried and has returned to live in Devon with her husband Tim. Debra and Tim adore living in the Westcountry and particularly enjoy the surf and stunning countryside.

For more information visit www.debrasearle.com.